ESSENCES OF WISDOM

ESSENCES OF WISDOM

ALDIVAN TORRES

Canary Of Joy

Contents

1 Essences of Wisdom   1

I

Essences of Wisdom

Essences of wisdom
Aldivan Teixeira Torres

Author: Aldivan Teixeira Torres
©2018-Aldivan Teixeira Torres
All rights reserved
This book, including all parts of it, is copyrighted and may not be reproduced without the author's permission, resold or transferred.

Aldivan Teixeira Torres, natural of Brazil, is a consolidated writer in various genres. So far, it's got titles published in nine languages. Since early, he's always been a lover of the art of writing, consolidated a professional career from the second semester of 2013. You wait with your writings to contribute to Brazilian culture, awakening the pleasure of reading in those who are not yet in habit. Your mission is to conquer the heart of each of your readers. In addition to literature, its main tastes are music, travel, friends, family and the very pleasure of living. For literature, equality, fraternity, justice, dignity and honor of human being always" is his motto.

Dedication and thanks

I dedicate this little book to all the souls thirsty for knowledge and wisdom. Let us take ourselves by the right moment seeking to learn from the creator these little lessons because it all comes from him.

I thank the lord of my life first, my family, my friends and admirers of my work as a writer. I'm happy for this new project.

Introduction

Essences of wisdom brings in itself an invitation so that you deepen in your spiritual father's knowledge. Through your observations and direct advice, the goal is to transform your reality and push it for good. Have a good read!

Texts

1. we are spiritual and carnal beings. In the spiritual part, we are impregnated of such magnetism that we can absorb the bad and good things others desire us. To avoid bad things, look for spiritual protection of light beings, and they will rid you of all kinds of traps. To attract good things, seek to maintain worldly values, a generous and fair ethic beyond a constant charity assisting the neediest. Always remember the law of return, which is supreme in the universe.
2. Stop this time running against time searching for material goods. Just seek what it takes to survive you and your family. The power and the overpaid money will only

bring you harm. See the millionaire's example? He lives in chains behind powerful walls, aiming to protect his fortune and his life from thieves. He practically has no social life, he can't walk on the street freely, he can't go to a beach with his family and live full of fear. Is that what you want for your life? Think carefully if it's not better to have a simple life, but be totally free.

3. At your command, worlds were created, natural elements and creatures. He alone is enough for all eternity. What seems impossible to man he can accomplish with strong hand and hope for his best project for our lives because it is truly pure and complete love. Let us deliver, therefore, our dreams in the right direction and work to be worthy of your mercy.

4. You are a one God. However, there are many ways to reach him. How do I know if I'm on the right track? Check the works and if these are good, represents a divine side. However, remember that the fact that you have a guidance does not give you the right to despise others.

5. Don't think God is an old bearded man living across the horizon. God has multiple faces presenting itself in its creatures, making address on the worthiest. Therefore, every good work comes from him, from his infinite generosity and mercy. You can also be represented by a legion of light warriors because that's exactly what he is, a union of the luminous forces. To please him, always seek to grow his commandments passed through his prophets. He who lives the reality of the Lord is always happier.

6. God is infinite love. The proof of this is their miracles throughout history for humanity, being the greatest of them the birth and resurrection of Jesus Christ. Let us enjoy this gift granted and honor our mission on Earth, objectively to be prepared for his return.

7. The worst karma is to insist on actions that bring no satisfactory results to anyone. If you want to avoid helping the next one, don't mess with it. Distilling your poison, you'll only be able to regress spiritually and sink into a dark abyss that you may not be

able to leave. Think well of the consequences of your actions.

8. Have a good mental disposition. You should know that if you have to practice good you will be tuned to good things, and consequently, you will see pure light. It's just liked the Lord said, hit and be opened, search and find yourself. This is one of the secrets of true happiness.

9. Everything we're looking for is not a logical explanation. The word of order is faith that you can believe and live, a reality that many people run from. Can you see love? No, but you can feel it. The same thing happens to the benign forces of the universe, they're always there for us, and we don't even realize it.

10. '"Know wisely, recognize the true friend. A true friend is the one who's with you in good times and bad times. He's the one who doesn't get tired of guiding you and even fighting you when you do something wrong. He is the one who cares about his well-being and seeks as far as possible to be present at the most important moments of his exis-

tence. Friend may be the Lord, his parents, his family, neighbors, or even unknown.
11. '"Understand your importance and position. Recognize yourself as the son of God and try to understand your performance in the universe. You should know that by your side has a loving father willing to fight for his happiness. But you want to do the same to yourself? Or will you give up on the obstacles? The way we act is essential to succeed.
12. The wisdom of a man is not measured by age. It shows itself through consolidated works throughout life. It's certain that the unreasonable does not sustain time, while the wise remains among the great. Once, right, someone told me that wisdom is as great as the intensity of our happiness, and I believe that is a great truth.
13. Along life, we are guided by carnal and spiritual masters. Its good wisdom to always hear them to follow a quiet, successful path on Earth. In return, they also learn from us in a multiple relationship. This proves the following jargon: "No one is so perfect that

he can't learn, or ignorant enough that he can't teach him enough."

14. What Jesus Christ proposes to our lives is a sincere contrition to the truth and his commandments. By renouncing our individuality, we may finally have the opportunity to forget our most inner pains and erase our sins.

15. If you are agreeing with the will of the Lord, you will know his word to which you will produce in contentment, tranquility and spiritual wisdom.

16. Everything has to be just right. Knowing how to talk and know how to understand each other's motives without any judgment makes you a good friend.

17. The essence of meditation must be applied in every stress situation, opening up the possibilities of resolution of a major problem without despair.

18. ' Work the good virtues itself so that they become extensive and deep as the ocean. In an analogue, avoid the bad things, suppressing them so that they have no more action in their life.

19. Be a guide to the ignorant, the same way you would help a blind man cross the street. Acting like this, the Lord will enlarge his wisdom by making the impossible possible.
20. ' don't allow day-to-day routine to produce disbelief in you. Always grow faith, and your efforts will be rewarded by generating consistent fruits.
21. ' the secret of knowledge is to follow the Lord's teachings. He will make the righteous wells of intelligence with knowledge, capable of knowing all things.
22. The sting of death will not be able to destroy love nor dignity of man. They will take you with you wherever you go because wherever your treasure is there will be your heart too.
23. The enemy struggles to block the path of the faithful, but they have a powerful lawyer who directed all doubts along with their father. He'll lead us to a land where milk and honey runs.
24. The family is our greatest good. When she's in crisis, we must try in every way to rescue her.
25. Do the good works and in return, you will

receive honor, success and happiness. There's no magic formula, no path ready to be a fair one. It is for each to discover in their reality the best way to cooperate for a better universe by honoring their mission on Earth. Be patient and tolerant in every situation keeps you controlling your life. Feel the spiritual aspect of the universe, associating with it, searching for something else. This force is called God and is ready to assist you in every moment of your life.

26. Notice the power and love of the creator. Whoever created the universe through a simple word is capable of doing a lot for you. Don't be so depressed. Its importance is too great for the balance of the planet, regardless of the degree of its responsibility. Make the little things great opportunities of knowledge.

27. Try to be a full-time citizen of good. You know, it's no sacrifice to be kind, give good advice, do a charity, be a companion, watch the sick, have a religious commitment, make it worth your rights and duties. Being an apostle of good is not an obligation because

each has its own free will, but it must be a goal for those who crave happiness in this world.

28. ' You know the secret of happiness? Keep your mind off the world's runs. Modernity and its technological devices revolutionized our way of living and communication between people. However, there comes a moment when it drowns us. So, if you could just leave them for a few moments, you'll feel something new, a completely abundant peace. Do that and see how satisfying it is for your mental well-being.

29. How do I know God? How to interpret your desire in our lives? First, it's important to rule out fake conventions usually accepted by most people. Don't expect the spiritual father to be distant in a chair made of gold. The Lord of the armies is in the slums, in the hospitals, in the nursing home, in the family unions, with you, and everywhere you are invoked. The spirit is that tiny little voice inside that advises you and drives you. So, thinking like this makes it a lot easier to un-

derstand you understanding your role in the world. Never stop following your intuition.

30. The driver plays a special role of great responsibility before God. He's responsible for driving vehicles, moving people from side to side. So, you need to take some care of yourself, don't take any drugs before you drive, walk at a moderate speed, so you can control the car in case of an eventuality and respect the laws of traffic. Take your time to reach the destination because time is a relative law.

31. You who are a retired old man or young man without a fixed job seek to occupy your mind with creative things. The important thing is to feel useful in some activity that provides pleasure and recognition. Take this as a good example of my case, I'm a writer, a public employee and a housewife with each of you taking up a space in my schedule. I also know people who have three fixed jobs, studies, and still work at home. Although not to be highly recommended such a load of work, the worst would be to be stagnant waiting for a miracle to happen in your life.

That's not how it works because we only succeed if we stick to our projects. With a good dedication, we can wait for God's blessing to help fulfill our plans.

32. If you want something done right, do it yourself. Don't expect the other one as the most capable of doing it for you. Be proactive, taking the reins of the space-time line in your story.

33. While the foolish uses its strength to oppress the righteous, this preserves wisdom and submission to the Lord. In the right time, the second will rise from hierarchy and stay among the great ones. In return, the first will harvest the fruits of its foolishness.

34. The lie has two points of view. On a temporarily calms the heart by making us believe in a world full of fairy tales. But you don't sustain yourself by falling on land. When that happens, there's a great inevitable pain. That's when we realize the best of all things is the truth, as hard as it is. In fact, the heart of God reigns and establishes, for justice lies in it.

35. Curse the slander and the slander. If you throw your tongue out or else the whole body will be burned in the dark outside. Why don't you mind your own business? If you want to criticize, look at yourself first and recognize your faults. So, who are you to judge the next one?
36. This is the promise of Jesus to all those who follow his commandments. Come be a part of this new spiritual reality, reminding yourself that no longer requires any painful sacrifice on your part because it was consummated on the cross.
37. The sky is the set of countless spiritual realities. We can also say there's no specific path to reach God. Each man is a path according to his peculiarity and as your worthiness will have the proper spiritual plan to his evolution.
38. Most entrances are our subconscious creating by generating the fear in facing them. As hard as the problem is, you know there's a solution for him. There's just no way to die.
39. give the Lord glory for all the good that happened in his life. He is a loving, generous

father who reigns in our existence. Never make the mistake of assigning God the responsibility of bad things. God has nothing to do with this. Fortune cases are consequences of our choices generated by free will. Be fair in your analysis.

40. All there is the Lord's manifestation, giving honor and glory to his name. Perfect are their laws and straight are their paths. That's why he's the Lord of the Armies.
41. Do your work with dedication and claw and behold you will have a highlighted position. Never use your position or influence to harm anyone because justice will reach you wherever you are.
42. Try to do periodic cleaning and cleaning up the body and the soul. They're cycle ends, necessary to clear your mind to reach higher flights. Remember that grudge and sin keep you away from God.
43. Plant and harvest the deserved fruits of your work. So, it also happens to our works because we only get what we give. If your works are good, the results will be too.
44. cult good values in such a way to follow the

commandments left by the Holy Spirit. It's a hard way, but it's worth it because it's going to be your lifeline.

45. The best way to praise the Lord is to help with acts and words the neediest in this world.

46. Nobody knows God but their beloved children. It is through them that we can understand a little of the greatness of the heart of the heavenly father. Basically, their laws are summed up in commandments and in the laws of common sense. Follow the good ethics and then all your jobs will be blessed. That doesn't mean your life will be easy. Our passage on Earth is a constant challenge, and a common sense of control is essential for us not to lose our course. Good luck to all my brothers in the heart!" Oh, my God.

47. Despite the greatness and the extent of the universe, nothing goes unnoticed according to the creator. With sovereign order and glory, he acts in every dimension that exists, represented by his messengers. As for him, it's an incognito for most people. But to me, he's not. I knew his face, his kindness and

protection at the most difficult time of my life, a time when I call the darkest night of the soul. It was a period of sin and removal of good that inspired me to write the second chapter of my main series. Though sad, confused and complicated I learned and was prepared by the divine for a larger mission which is exactly, to participate in the literary world with construction of the human being to evolve towards the father's path. This project is still embryonic, but gradually, it will draw my mission on Earth. I hope I can count on your support in this important exchange of knowledge. Thank you very much, everyone who accompanies me!"

48. There's no way a man can be aware of what happens or knowledge of his father's property. As much as you research and seek, you will never achieve the full truth. This happens so that our Lord will be respected forever and ever. We must submit and surrender to this immense creator power because it knows exactly what's best for us. Do as I do and turn the page of your life.

49. just as the river water follows the current,

let it be carried by fate. You want to avoid swimming against the current because this will only bring you bad results. Fight for your goals, but know that the final word comes from God.

50. There are many who call themselves wise, but in truth everyone is mere fools. In front of God, there is no power, science or wisdom. All good things come from him pouring himself for the mortals they deserve. But you never want to be more than you really are. It's called humility.

51. All the understanding of infinity is in God. Infinite wisdom, infinite love, mercy, generosity and protection. To be human, you just have a conscience of your actions seeking to repair your mistakes by aiming spiritual evolution.

52. Many scholars study the limits of the universe unsuccessful. Why not study your limits? This way, looking for something palpable gets easier to analyze relationships between each other and the others. This is much more important than looking for vain things that are not in our reach.

53. The only great is the Lord, who deserves by rights all honor, glory and worship. From the sky, he pours his grace to his faithful of his heart. Do, for, works compatible with this gift.
54. ' If we seek good works, our life fills with positive vibrations, optimism and happiness. Otherwise, the dark night takes full of our soul. Even though this last choice is bad, the human being is totally free to decide its path.
55. The largest of people becomes ungrateful not to recognize the good deeds of their spiritual father in his life, remaining in the immense quest of wanting more and more. This is all fleeting, being a useless race. To man, just worry about the present, for tomorrow only God belongs.
56. In established are the gifts of the Lord and few who take advantage of them. Be like the example of the good servant who grows good talent and multiplies them by three. Don't act like the ungrateful servant who buries his gifts.
57. The servant is no greater than your lord, but

if you do a good job, you can conquer your trust and be considered your son.

58. I have a crowd at my disposal that worships me and glorifies me. So, despite the enemy struggling, he can't succeed in his projects. So, it happens for my sovereignty to be respected by all.

59. I created everything in the visible and invisible universe. All owe me life, honor, glory and worship. This is nothing more than sincere gratitude. However, many prefer to go their own way not listening to my inner advice getting away from my convivial. Still, I have hopes that with the circumstances, I can regain your soul. However, I let you completely free to decide what you want because I love you with all my heart, thought and soul.

60. Let life led you to more defined paths. Think, think, and dare. Valuate the good things in life. Forgive and love more.

61. There is no justice and mercy greater than mine. I act this way because I know exactly what goes on in the bottom of every human heart. Don't try to fool me with false

promises because it only lights my wrath. You want to avoid abusing my patience, either because you won't like it. My hand is very heavy when I want it.

62. Beauty is important when it comes from the outside in. Don't get attached to the illusion of a pretty figure, though, poor spiritually speaking. All that is land passes by just staying the good works.

63. Sing to the Lord a new chant full of respect and worship. Nothing fairer than praising the people who raised us and continually protect us from the dangers.

64. Love is the most creative force existing, which brings us closer to God." Love the next one without expecting retribution and without expectations.

65. Nobody lives without dreams. Look, for, plan, act and cultivate your desires. Being noble, they will become reality for their effort.

66. Although there is a hierarchy in human relations, we must not always obey our superiors. It says the public servant must be strictly the law. If it is not mandatory, we

are not required to obey, even if it is the president of the Republic to order us.

67. I met my spiritual father in one of the hardest moments of my life. He was the only one who trusted me when I was thrown into a deep, dark abyss. Through his angel, he pulled me out of there and started teaching a little of his values. With time watching around me, I could learn even more about him. I can tell you that he is a father, generous, human, companion, supportive, tolerant, fair and merciful father who really cares about us. He adopted me as a son and turned me into a worthy man because I gave him my cause. Do that too, and you'll see how your life will change completely.

68. Although God is the most supreme being in the universe, we can approach him as children. Adopting moral values and consistent ethics, we can be proud of being called "Son of God" in its most meaning ".

69. Always believe in your potential, fighting bravely for your dreams. God gave us enough wisdom to build our identity and transform relations. To succeed, it is neces-

sary, for first we have the spirit of peace and charity with us. The good you want for yourself, do others, and then you'll have found the secret of happiness.

70. Keep up in any situation. As much trouble as you have, raise your head and move on. Find solutions and the Lord God will help you. Remember that the impossible does not exist for him to perform in his truly remarkable miracles.

71. learn to be happy. Happiness is nothing more than a conscience of spirit. Find what you lack in nature, in relationship with yourself, with God and his partner. Accept yourself with your faults and qualities by not creating expectations towards others. This will prevent unnecessary suffering.

72. Never compliment a man for his beauty because this is a passenger. What truly matters about him is character, moral and ethical concepts which he will lead to his entire life.

73. Measure your words, so you don't hurt each other. If you can't help, don't get in the way of letting the other be happy in your own way.

74. Through its power and sovereignty, controls the universe with an iron hand. Even though he's so powerful and so big, he cares about every one of us. He makes you want to join his kingdom in communion with his blessed children. However, this choice is yours only because of free will. He'll never make you love him.
75. God's mercy is as great as the extent of the universe. However, this is not a justification to continue sinning. Straighten up as soon as you have a happy life.
76. The structure of the universe is magnificent, with every element of this performing an important function. So, it occurs in the spiritual and carnal kingdoms. Soon, when you feel depressed, think your presence is significant to someone.
77. The work is fundamental for human being to grow up and have dignity. Run away from the godforsaken mind, go to the gym, study the healthy and pleasurable activities, walk, listen to music, travel, travel with friends, talk to people of trust, go regularly to the gym, study the healthy and pleasurable ac-

tivities, pray hard for you and your next and exclude your life, which makes you ill. Acting like this, the possibilities of you feeling peaceful and happy will be greater.
78. Cheers your heart in such a way that life will be light. Take away your mind, all that contributes to sorrow and pain. Forget hate, resentment, loss, and failure. You think taking a new path, things will get better for you. Remember, every time there's a way and an exit except death.
79. which makes you a warrior is not the number of wars that won, but how many obstacles have overcome.
80. Education is key to insert yourself into the work market and build an ethical and reputable personality.
81. Make your passage on earth a moment of worship to the Lord. Building a set of good works, your soul will achieve the light and peace necessary for your welfare.
82. There's no middle ground. Either you're on the side of good or the dark side. This is the consequence of free will give to man.
83. Being a hero is not getting something fan-

tastic. Being a hero is fighting for your dreams in a country where cultural investment is precarious. But you must resist and continue fighting.

84. Give wings your will. Release your inner self so that the hindrances of the way don't make you give up. Even in the face of a great difficulty, keep faith.
85. seek humility and simplicity. The sublime comes from that essence of being. Show in your little size the size of your greatness.
86. The value of man is in his authenticity. Being authentic is to have a defined pattern of behavior with honest values. I strongly recommend the following of the commandments and the divine laws given by God to their prophets.
87. Who truly loved or loved? You must reflect and observe everything around us. Let's say we recognize love through signs. The people who really love you are always there for you in good and bad times, even if occasionally you're not the full reason. Whoever loves you will discover your worst, and yet will continue to love you and identify with your

faults and qualities. Whoever loves you always supports your slips, doesn't wait for the right time to hug you and say they love you. Whoever loves you will know how to forgive and reciprocate will deserve to be forgiven in your failures. Whoever loves you will always believe you in every situation. So, never let the loved one down.

88. True love is rare to find, it's much harder than winning the federal lottery." Still, never give up. Love yourself first so that others may have a chance to love you.

89. Happiness is something that comes from the inside out and not the other way around. Happiness is enjoying life is at work, on trips, with family, friends, reading a book, writing a story or fighting for a dream. The important thing is to keep moving forward, even in defeats.

90. God never comes from us. At no time, he stops taking care of our pain and difficulties, proving such a true fatherly love. Instead of asking him for things, thank him for what he has.

91. Watch the world. Wolves are lurking around

his life around every corner of the street across the street. They just want to see their disgrace, practically no hope for a world populated by evil creatures. In return to this behavior, do it differently. Take care of yourself, your family and your close so that everyone recognizes your works. Be an apostle of good always, and then the kingdom of God will be a reality in your life.

92. Examples of that are faith, God, and love. They all exist, but on earth we don't have a clear view of it. Just try to understand them through their reactions.

93. ' There is no other force or power worthy of admiration in the entire universe. So don't have idols before you.

94. Have meditation as a good practice of relaxation and to meet with yourself. Do this activity whenever you're looking for some peace.

95. Professor, keep in mind that your profession is noble and honorable. Through education, all professionals are formed, from the president to the cleaner. So be proud of what you do.

96. ' Ground his kindness and generosity by assisting all living beings. Don't do good out of obligation, do it for feeling good without waiting for retribution. The honors and glories will be given to you in the kingdom of heaven.
97. Nothing or anyone can stop their happiness. If you are on the side of good, you will surely receive the blessings of heaven so that your life progresses in every way. So, stay calm and faithful always.
98. before the good God you have value and for your deserving you receive divine protection.' Knows to enjoy this so that you can achieve all your goals.
99. Where are your treasures? Think exactly what's good for you. In my case, my happiness comes from work, from the living, from the reading, from my books, from the travels, of my good works and of life itself. If you thought similar to me, then your cause before God is already won, for your path will overflow in the kingdom of the father. Their happiness, harmony, and peace will prevail in its existence forever and ever.

100. The humble will be exalted, while the proud will be humiliated. Two opposites that truly shows how father wants us to act before him. The most recommended is to try to follow the example of Jesus, which left us the perfect man model.

101. Here's the mystery of faith. If you believe in the spiritual forces of good, you believe in me and my father. We are in joint the force that coordinates the universes with authority, power, and sovereignty. Nothing gets out of our control, even when the man feels big. Nothing can defeat us or our servants. We are the initial stone of everything that exists and seeks men committed to our cause. Come be a part of this spiritual reality.

102. Do you feel hungry and thirsty? Do you feel restless, disturbed and misunderstood? Are you feeling insecure and unhappy? The solution to all these problems is in me and my father. Our laws and commandments are true food, drink, and peace for your soul. Fear not in the darkness, betrayal, the evil, and wickedness of men, for before you, the

lamb of Israel. I am the king of kings and Lord of Lords, and nothing runs me to power. Believe me, in my kindness and mercy. Do your part and I will bless you?

103. Find love." Find to love God, your family and the next without waiting to reciprocate. Behold, love and charity can erase any kind of sin, as severe as it may be. Always Love and without measures. This way, you will truly be my son.

104. Knows to deal with the criticism as hard as they are. Try to extract something positive from the words that hurt your soul painfully. This is part of your maturing process and evolution as a human and professional being. Just don't accept that you step on your dignity or be unfair with your work performed.

105. Keep performing your daily jobs with no greater concerns. If you're doing right, you have nothing to worry about. I promise you the aid in good times and bad, in such a way that wounded tongues don't harm your life. By the way, don't even care about them. They seek in each other's life the glow that

doesn't belong in theirs. They are worthy of your sincere pity.

106. Don't bother with the mistake. He comes to show his faults, and it's up to you to fix them so that something similar doesn't happen again. Mistakes lead to the right.

107. In a distress, try to vent and give your feelings away. This is completely healthy, and it will do your soul good. Never keep in your heart what's bad and what brings you sorrows.

108. Have mercy on socially marginalized. Examples of these are the homeless, the smallest street, the orphans, the druggies, and the hookers. Try to help them somehow, materially or spiritually. However, you know, the slicker who takes advantage of our goodwill to take advantage. To these, pray God gives you some sense.

109. Be persistent in prayer, seeking to contact God in times programmed or in case of need anywhere. He'll always be willing to listen to you and help you in the best way.

110. learn the law of life and teach the younger. Try to demonstrate the kingdom of God and

his implications in daily life, frightening that always worth being a good, honest man.
111. God damn whoever speaks ill of you or the beings of light in any degree. The Lord God is good and fair, proving it through his works. He's a real father because he gives sun and rain for good and bad. Now to be grateful to him for all the good that happened in his life and never attribute bad things to his action.
112. Run from the traps of your mind. Not always what, we think, is true. We have to analyze everything coldly so that we can judge a case fairly.
113. The essence of good consists of love, mercy, generosity, tolerance, charity, generosity, generosity, generosity, generosity, peace, protection, and understanding. The essence of wisdom is to hear the next and understand their reasons.
114. We're made of dust and for him, we'll return. Why then many carry a pride like they're invulnerable and unattainable? Recognize your little and act so that the Lord protect you from all evil. To do good.

115. All things follow a previous order. For each person, a specific talent and a mission that can be up to you. In the same way, the gifts are distributed according to the deserving of each.
116. Being miserable for his poverty of spirit, for his avarice and his pride. In return, being become beautiful through your generosity, tenderness, and love.
117. Stop bothering my father every day for his personal drama. Don't be selfish, ask for your next one, God will look at your problems.
118. know the good work and the benefactor. Be grateful for everything God has given you in the present to build a beautiful future.
119. ' The true religion are good works and attitudes. They're the ones who will credentialing you into my kingdom.
120. Thank God requires a great effort. When we made a mistake, it's a great opportunity to analyze our projects and get the possible solutions. Recognizing sin is the first step to forgiveness and consequent remission.
121. Man's doom is to want to be like the creator,

becoming self-sufficient. You have to admit, we came from the dust and for him, we came back. All people are subject to diseases, accidents, mistakes, and misfortunes. Then why want to be big without actually being it? Let's be humbler and seek to fulfill the Lord's word.

122. The secret of happiness consists of not having much expectation towards others and seek to live on the honest line of honor. The righteous will always be blessed.

123. All life forms come from the creator. For that reason, you see no reason to discriminate anyone. We are equal before you in every way.

124. You are sovereign in the entire universe. We can see this work of the creator in the elements and creatures that make up the world visible and invisible. Through it, we can admire the true benefactor of everything.

125. Watching nature and its natural laws, we can conclude that we are part of a whole larger."

126. Be observant, but try not to interfere with the other.

127. Give alms to those who really need it. Don't let yourself be fooled by the smart-asses of this world who use their kindness to raise advantages. This crime is called an embezzlement.
128. God is everywhere and especially in the good people. Know your sovereign will about your life, collaborating for a planet where people are more human.
129. My mercy, kindness, and understanding are unfathomable. Fear not my wrath, just do so that your good deeds redeem your mistakes.
130. To be sublime is to be political in the way of treating people is to forgive the next even if he doesn't deserve it, it's to love and be loved in a world more and more full of evil, is to always believe in a good future when you work in the present. Being sublime is also working every day with honesty, honorable and dignity to strengthen the family bond. To be sublime is to be simple because only these will inherit the best position in my father's kingdom.
131. Born, live and die. Autumn, summer, spring and winter. All of this is phases, and in each

one of them we must know to behave objectively, fully success.
132. In this world and the next, we only get exactly what we deserve.
133. If you want to be the greatest, follow my cross and make yourself a servant of your neighbor, for royalty comes from small.
134. Stop making excuses to yourself. Try to integrate yourself to a good religiosity in such a way that your actions are a reflection of what you believe. Long live your authenticity.
135. Stop blaming me for your mistakes. Do a criterion's analysis of your trajectory and all your actions. There will come a time when you'll find out you're the only one responsible for your victories and defeats. Let's just say I'm your supporter.
136. stay away from any kind of drug. Besides causing dependence, this kind of thing gives you a false sense of being happy.
137. Each must do his part for his personal and world progress. Acting as a team, we can achieve consistent victories.
138. we must revitalize and control our emotions

in such a way that we do not harm each other. However, for us to reach this internship is required knowledge of yourself and the surrounding middle.

139. ' Follow my example that the earth be blessed and life remains for a long time.

140. Even if the man lives in palace acting in the position of king, nothing will be before God if he can't keep love, charity and honorable. What saves the soul of man is his good works and values. Therefore, power, influence, and wealth mean nothing before the Creator.

141. Continue to live. Don't let the sadness and the grudge bite your heart at any moment. If the other one hurt you, forgive for your own good. Follow your life looking to accomplish a good job on every possible sphere.

142. seek education as a primary source of wisdom. Without it, nothing is built, nothing progresses. Instead of leaving it as an inheritance of material goods, leave it as an inheritance to your children.

143. Nothing happens by chance. Every person who enters your life does it for some reason.

Try to understand the signs of fate to build a happy walk.

144. No use wasting your precious time with people who don't deserve it. Step away from the darkness and gather around your thoughts and positive elements. Good attracts good.

145. Exclude his life the bad times, the bad influences, the envy, the perversion, the chase, the sadness. Love more, give more, believe more in yourself and in God, always having a positive point of view even with bad facts. Hooray!

146. Do so that your attitudes and words influence others positively."'

147. Try not to isolate yourself. The man is a social being who depends on the other to survive.

148. Be clear in your observations, not leaving shore for false interpretations.

149. be always optimistic, never giving up your dreams.

Part II

The Life Sense

Silly is the one who seeks incessantly to find a meaning for life. Despite all your efforts, you'll waste time, money, and you'll still produce stress and mental tiredness. Simply because there is no explanation for the existence. Meanwhile, man should worry about other things more pertinent. Set up projects and dreams. Find them without harming anyone. Allied to it, promote good and charity. When man surrenders himself into the hands of God, his desires and aspirations are fulfilled. That's the crop-crop logic, or the Return Act. This is the most important law visible to humans. So don't ever say God's bad will. It was you with your hands that got the wrong hands, and now you're harvesting the damages. We are our judges.

The current situation

Greed, envy, the thirst for justice, the incomprehension, the disaster, the competition, the contentment, the disrespect, and intolerance made men less human. So much so that there's hardly purity on the face of the earth. Or few good remaining are the ones who remain happy. Welfare is directly proportional to goodness, honesty, love, generosity, and faith in God. Being good, all your plans will be blessed by the deity. Even the bad guys, there's always a chance to start over. Because God is the father of everyone.

Recognize yourself, little man

Who am I? I didn't come from the dust? I won't return to him, either? We must meditate on this maximum to grow humility on every occasion. The man is great for his attitudes and works. Immediately, he became a divine instrument. Good does not attribute to a name. It's a manifestation of the creator among mortals. Through us, the writing of life is taking shape. Everything is written and must happen.

The Unwise

Evil produces more and more hate and unhappiness. Those who are busy harming each other are true human worms. They are true sons of Satan, the fallen angel. To us children of God, all remains to ask for protection from the beings of light. Surely, with God's company, we shall fear no evil. Though I walk on the dark valley, with your art. If we have a thousand opponents, God sends ten grand in our protection. Good is stronger and will always prevail as long as we surrender to your will and company.

The Fate

Life leads us to unexpected circumstances. In our time on Earth, we live in pain, sorrows, joys, disappointments, accomplishments, which means, dichotomous situations. Each of these events, it's going to strengthen us and preparing us for the after facts. A pure heart becomes mature. Still, we don't own your nose. Sometimes things happen in such a way that makes us make important decisions. Often, one dream replaces another. To this greater force, I call destiny or predestination. All these forces are commanded by a higher power that only wants our good. You could say that's a good thing.

The company of the Angels

The angels are our journey companions on Earth. Intuitively, they suggest good deeds and thoughts. In front of the dangers, they help us. On difficult matters, they advise us. You should know to talk to your angel, better understanding God's will. Surely, this partnership will be more fruitful.

The end

www.ingramcontent.com/pod-product-compliance
Lightning Source LLC
LaVergne TN
LVHW020443080526
838202LV00055B/5322